The Special Ingredient in Puerto Rican Cookery

Sabor Boricua: A Culinary Journey through Puerto Rican Delights

Clari Diaz

Gotham Books

30 N Gould St.
Ste. 20820, Sheridan, WY 82801
https://gothambooksinc.com/

Phone: 1 (307) 464-7800

© 2023 *Clari Diaz*. All rights reserved.

No part of this book may be reproduced, stored in a retrieval system, or transmitted by any means without the written permission of the author.

Published by Gotham Books (November 1, 2023)

ISBN: 979-8-88775-650-9 (H)
ISBN: 979-8-88775-648-6 (P)
ISBN: 979-8-88775-649-3 (E)

Because of the dynamic nature of the Internet, any web addresses or links contained in this book may have changed since publication and may no longer be valid.

The views expressed in this work are solely those of the author and do not necessarily reflect the views of the publisher, and the publisher hereby disclaims any responsibility for them.

I liked to dedicate this book to my friend and partner
Dickie Hernandez

He has brought the overall experience of cooking for friends as a way to strengthen social bonds, share experiences, and create a sense of togetherness and fun through the universal language of food. It's a gesture that brings joy and connection, making it an integral part of human interaction and friendship and family.

Get ready for a mouthwatering adventure! This book is like a treasure trove of cherished recipes that have a special place in my heart, and they're about to find a place in yours too. Imagine the aroma of those dishes that take you back to the joyful moments spent in the kitchen with loved ones.

These recipes are like secret family heirlooms passed down through generations, but don't worry, we've got a little twist in store. As each generation adds their own flair and pizzazz, these recipes keep getting better and better while holding onto their core ingredients and traditions. It's a culinary journey that brings people together, igniting a passion for cultural exchange and learning.

Now, here's the exciting part: these recipes might not taste the same for everyone, but that's where the magic happens. We want you to sprinkle your creativity and personality into each dish. Go ahead, add your "special ingredient" and watch the flavors come alive in your kitchen. Suddenly, your version becomes a hit with your family and friends, and they'll be begging for your recipe secrets.

In this delightful book, you'll find a collection of recipes straight from my kitchen. They're infused with that one-of-a kind "special ingredient" that makes them truly unique. So, put on your apron, unleash your inner chef, and get ready to create unforgettable memories and flavors that'll have everyone asking for seconds. Let's dive in and make cooking an adventure to savor!

Before we begin with these wonderful recipe creations, allow me a moment to describe my culinary delights from my beautiful island paradise. Living in Puerto Rico is like being in a culinary paradise! The abundance of freshly grown produce on this island is nothing short of a hidden treasure waiting to be discovered. It's like finding a pot of gold at the end of a rainbow!

Let's talk about the starchy delights that grace my table. Malanga, plantains, yuca (cassava), and pana (breadfruit) are the real MVPs. They bring such a wonderful depth of flavor and texture to any dish. Whether it's a crispy plantain toston or a comforting mashed malanga, these ingredients make every meal a memorable experience.

But wait, there's more! The variety of fruit here is simply mind-blowing. Coconuts, mangos, pineapples, and papayas are like nature's sweet ambassadors, adding a burst of tropical goodness to any recipe. Just imagine the sheer delight of sinking your teeth into a juicy mango or savoring the refreshing taste of a perfectly ripened pineapple. It's pure bliss!

Now, let's spice things up a bit with the herbs. Cilantro, oregano, and sweet basil are just a few of the magical herbs that make Puerto Rican cuisine sing. They bring a savory kick to our dishes and allow us to create our own unique sofrito base. I mean, who doesn't love the aroma of fresh herbs wafting through the kitchen? It's like a symphony of flavors dancing in the air!

And let's take a moment to give a round of applause to the avocado. Oh, the avocado! It deserves a category of its own. This creamy, green gem adds the perfect finishing touch to any dish. From guacamole to salads, even soups, the avocado brings a burst of freshness that takes the flavor to a whole new level. It's like a little slice of heaven on your plate!

Living in Puerto Rico means being surrounded by a vibrant tapestry of flavors and ingredients. Each meal is a celebration of the land and the love poured into the food. So, grab a seat at my table, and let's embark on a gastronomic adventure that will leave you craving for more.

Table of Contents

Rice With Pigeon Peas 1

Clari's Chicken Fricassee 3

Clari's Lasagna 5

Clari's Savory Sausage And Peppers 7

Yuca Con Mojito 9

Steak Smothered With Onions 11

Chicken Scarpariello A La Clari 13

Pork Country Ribs Cooked In Air Fryer 15

Pasteles Untraditional Puerto Rican Style 18

Meatballs With Pasta 23

Sweet Potato Casserole 25

Marisa's Tomato Soup 27

Puerto Rican Shrimp Stew 29

Breaded Breast Of Chicken 31

Cooking White Rice 33

Tasty Mini Cheesecakes 35

Arroz Con Dulce 37

Coquito 39

RICE WITH PIGEON PEAS
(Arroz con Gandules)
A Traditional Puerto Rican Dish

Ah, the delightful Arroz con Gandules! A taste of Puerto Rico's rich culinary heritage. And you've added a twist with the unexpected ingredient of beer! That's a fascinating story. Let's dive into the fun and explore this unique recipe together.

Here's the fun-filled recipe for your special Arroz con Gandules:

Ingredients:
- 2 cups of medium-grain rice
- 1 can of gandules (pigeon peas), drained and rinsed.
- 1 cup of beer (your choice of brand and flavor)
- 1 ½ cups of chicken stock
- 1 tablespoon of olive oil
- 1 onion finely chopped.
- 3 garlic cloves, minced.
- 1 green bell pepper, diced.
- 1 red bell pepper, diced.
- 1 tomato, diced.
- 1 packet of sazón seasoning (Puerto Rican seasoning blend)
- 1 teaspoon of ground cumin
- 1 teaspoon of dried oregano
- Salt and pepper to taste
- Fresh cilantro or parsley for garnish (optional)

Instructions:

1. In a large pot or caldero (traditional Puerto Rican cooking pot), heat the olive oil over medium heat. Add the chopped onion, minced garlic, and diced bell peppers. Sauté until they become soft and fragrant.
2. Add the diced tomato, sazón seasoning, ground cumin, dried oregano, salt, and pepper to the pot. Stir well and let the flavors combine for a couple of minutes.
3. Now, it's time to add the star ingredient! Pour in the cup of beer and 1 ½ cups of chicken stock and let it simmer for a minute or two, allowing the flavors to meld together.
4. Next, add the drained gandules (pigeon peas) to the pot. Give everything a good stir, ensuring that the ingredients are evenly mixed.
5. Add the rice to the pot and stir until it's well-coated with the flavorful mixture.
6. Once boiling, reduce the heat to low, cover the pot, and let it simmer for about 20-25 minutes, or until the rice is cooked and all the liquid has been absorbed.
7. Once the rice is ready, fluff it gently with a fork. If you like a bit of crispy goodness, you can let the bottom layer of rice toast a little by increasing the heat for a minute or two but be careful not to burn it!

8. Serve your delicious Arroz con Gandules hot, garnished with fresh cilantro or parsley, if desired. And voilà, you've created a unique twist on a beloved Puerto Rican dish!

Now, with your special ingredient of beer, your Arroz con Gandules is sure to have a distinctive flavor and an interesting story to share. Enjoy the dish with your loved ones and let the memories and laughter flow! But remember don't forget to add a slice of avocado to each plate!
Is there anything else I can assist you with or add a touch of fun to?

Serves: 6

CLARI'S CHICKEN FRICASSEE
(Cooked Puerto Rican Style)

Welcome to the world of Chicken Fricassee, where flavor and healing properties come together in a delightful dish. Let's dive into this recipe with a dash of fun and creativity!
But first, let's put on our imaginary chef hats and aprons and gather all the ingredients for our chicken adventure.

Ingredients for Chicken Fricassee:
- 4 Chicken Thighs
- 4 Wings
- 4 Legs
- Any combination of chicken pieces works, but it's best to use at least two types for maximum flavor. However, you can also stick with chicken thighs if that's your family's favorite.

Seasoning for Chicken (preferably one day before cooking):
- 1 ½ tsp adobo
- ½ tsp smoked paprika (the special ingredient that adds a unique flavor)
- 1 tsp garlic powder
- ½ tsp oregano leaves
- 1 tbs sazón (a delicious Puerto Rican seasoning blend)

For the Stew:
- 3 tbs olive oil
- ½ cup diced ham
- 3 medium-sized Idaho Potatoes, quartered.
- 1 tbs chopped cilantro
- ½ Red Pepper, diced
- ½ Spanish Onion, diced
- 3 Large Garlic Cloves, mashed in a pilon (mortar and pestle). Add 3 tbs of olive oil, 1 tbs of vinegar, and mix into a sauce.
- ½ cup of Tomato Sauce (garlic-based if possible)
- ½ cup of Merlot (the special ingredient that adds a touch of richness)
- ½ tsp of oregano leaves
- 1 Envelope of Sazón (a flavorful seasoning blend)
- 2 cups of Chicken stock
- 2 tbs of flour

Now that we have all the ingredients, let's embark on our Chicken Fricassee adventure!
1. Get ready for a flavor fiesta by marinating the chicken overnight in a mix of adobo, smoked paprika, garlic powder, oregano leaves, and sofrito. Let those seasonings work their magic in the fridge!

2. When the big cooking day arrives, heat up some olive oil in a pot or Dutch oven. Toss in diced ham and let it sizzle until it gets crispy and releases its mouthwatering flavors.
3. Time to introduce the marinated chicken to the pot! Brown those beauties on all sides until they turn a golden hue. This step is all about sealing in the juiciness and adding a delightful crunch.
4. Take a breather and temporarily remove the chicken from the pot. They need a little break before the grand reunion.
5. Now, it's vegetable party time! Add diced red pepper, diced Spanish onion, and a mashed garlic mixture to the pot. Sauté them until they soften up and fill your kitchen with a tantalizing aroma. Prepare for your taste buds to start dancing!
6. Bring the chicken back to the pot, along with any glorious juices they left behind. It's time to add the star ingredients: tomato sauce, Merlot (yes, we're adding a splash of wine for that extra pizzazz), oregano leaves, quartered potatoes, Scazon seasoning (don't forget the secret blend!), and chicken stock. Give it all a good stir, making sure the chicken gets cozy in that flavorful mixture. Oh, and a sprinkle of flour adds that special touch!
7. Let the pot work its simmering magic. Cover it up and let everything cook together for about 45 minutes. This is when the chicken becomes tender and soaks up all the irresistible flavors of the stew. It's a symphony of deliciousness!
8. Brace yourself for the miracle of healing properties that this stew possesses. One spoonful and everyone will feel like they've been touched by culinary magic. Prepare for smiles, warmth, and a table full of happy, satisfied bellies! Enjoy the enchantment, my friends!
9. Remember to add a slice of avocado to each dish to make the enchantment complete!

Serves: 6

CLARI'S LASAGNA

Get ready for a lasagna extravaganza that will leave your taste buds cheering! This mouthwatering dish has a story of its own, starting with teaching my mom the basics. But hold on tight because this dish took a twist of its own and became the superstar of all our family gatherings. Today, it has transformed into a masterpiece, and let me tell you, it's a creation straight from my culinary dreams!

Ingredients:
- 1 lb. lasagna, cooked to perfection.
- 1.5 lbs. fresh ricotta, oh so creamy
- 10 oz. shredded mozzarella, the cheesier, the better
- 6 oz. grated pecorino or romano cheese, for that perfect tangy kick
- 3 eggs, to bind the magic together.
- 1 handful of freshly chopped parsley, because we love that burst of freshness.

For the Meat Sauce:
- 4 links of Sweet Italian Sausage, casing removed.
- 2 links of Hot Italian Sausage, casing removed (our secret ingredient for that spicy kick!)
- 3-4 cloves of garlic, chopped with flair.
- 1/4 onion finely chopped.
- A drizzle of olive oil, for that sizzle
- One envelope of Sazón, because we love adding a touch of Latin flavor.
- 1/2 cup white wine (special ingredient for that extra oomph!)
- 3 jars of garlic and/or basil-based tomato sauce, because let's keep it saucy.
- 3 fresh basil leaves, chopped to perfection.

To create the meat sauce, we start by drizzling a little olive oil into a pan and adding the Italian sausages. Sauté them until they're gloriously browned, then add the garlic, onion, and white wine. Cook until the wine dances away, and finally, pour in the tomato sauce. Let it simmer and mingle with the flavors for about two hours. Oh, and don't forget to add those delightful basil leaves for that extra burst of freshness.

While your meat sauce is doing its thing, cook the lasagna sheets according to the package instructions. Once they're perfectly al dente, drain them and sprinkle a touch of olive oil to keep them from sticking together. Lay them out on wax paper in layers, like little lasagna stars getting ready for their grand performance.

Now, it's showtime! Preheat your oven to a toasty 400°F and get a big bowl ready for the cheese extravaganza. Mix together the ricotta cheese and eggs until they're singing in harmony. Throw in a handful of mozzarella and pecorino cheese and give them a whirl. Now, here comes the fun part: scoop in half a ladle of that incredible meat sauce and mix it all up. Sprinkle in the parsley, a pinch of salt, and a dash of black pepper for that extra pizzazz.

Grab a baking pan and spread two scoops of meat sauce evenly on the bottom. Now, it's time to layer like a lasagna maestro! Lay down three to four lasagna sheets, side by side, to cover the bottom of the pan. Pour two scoops of meat sauce on top, spreading it out like a saucy symphony. Add two to three scoops of the ricotta cheese mixture and spread it out evenly over the sauce and pasta. Sprinkle a heavenly handful of mozzarella and pecorino cheese on top and repeat these delicious layers until you reach the pinnacle of lasagna goodness.

For the final act, cover your lasagna masterpiece with two scoops of tomato sauce, and resist the urge to add cheese on top (we'll get to that later, promise!). It's showtime, folks! Time to bring your lasagna masterpiece to life and let the flavors party in the oven! Grab your trusty aluminum foil cape and cover your creation like a superhero protecting its secrets. Pop it in the oven and let the magic happen for a whole hour. Get ready for the anticipation to build as the aroma fills your kitchen.

Now, the grand finale awaits! Unleash your inner cheese ninja and remove the lasagna from the oven. It's time to sprinkle the remaining mozzarella and pecorino cheese on top like confetti raining down on a culinary celebration. Pop it back in the oven, this time without the foil, and let the cheese dance and melt for about 10 minutes. Keep an eye on it because you want that cheese to reach the perfect melty goodness.

Finally, the moment we've all been waiting for—remove your masterpiece from the oven and let it rest for a tantalizing 5 minutes. It's like letting the lasagna catch its breath before the grand finale. Grab your trusty knife and cut the lasagna into mouthwatering serving sizes, each one a delicious work of art. Now, it's time to gather your eager audience, your family and friends, and serve up this culinary masterpiece.

Get ready for a symphony of "oohs" and "ahhs" as they take their first bite. Brace yourself for the chorus of praises and the sheer delight that will light up their faces. This is the moment where all your hard work and culinary genius pay off. So, sit back, bask in the applause, and savor the satisfaction of creating a lasagna that will be remembered and cherished for years to come. Bravo!

Serves: 8

CLARI'S SAVORY SAUSAGE AND PEPPERS

Get ready for an Italian-Puerto Rican flavor fusion with this dish I've crafted over the years. It all started when I tasted sausage and peppers at a wedding and fell head over heels. I knew I had to master this recipe, and after much experimenting, I can proudly say I've made it my own. I even passed on the secrets to my daughter, Marisa, and her family can't get enough of it!

Here's what you'll need:

Ingredients:
- 8 Sweet Italian Sausages
- 6 Hot Italian Sausages
- 3 Garlic Cloves, sliced.
- 2 Red Peppers, julienne cuts
- ½ Spanish Onion, julienne cuts
- 1 tbsp of dry Oregano leaves
- 2 cups of low sodium chicken stock (keep ½ cup reserved for flour)
- 2 heaping tbsp of flour
- ¼ cup of prepared marinara sauce
- 1 envelope of Sazón powder
- ½ cup of merlot (our secret ingredient!)
- 1 tbsp of unsalted butter
- 1 tbsp of olive oil

Let's get cooking!
1. Heat up the olive oil in a large 12-inch frying pan. We're ready to rock!
2. Add the Italian sausages and sprinkle in the oregano. Let them sizzle and brown over low-medium heat, but don't forget to give them a little poke with a fork to release all that deliciousness into the pan.
3. Pour enough chicken stock into the pan to reach halfway up the sausages. This is where the magic happens!
4. Let the sausages simmer away over a very low flame for about 30 minutes. The aromas will start wafting through your kitchen, building up the excitement.
5. Once the sausages are cooked, remove them from the pan and let them cool down. They need a breather before joining the flavor party again.
6. Turn up the heat to a medium flame and let the liquid in the pan evaporate a little. We're getting the base ready for all those amazing ingredients to shine!
7. Time to add the peppers, onions, sofrito, sazón, and garlic to the pan. Let them dance around for about 16 minutes, infusing the air with their tantalizing scents. Then, add the

butter, merlot wine, flour mixed with ¼ cup of chicken stock, and watch as the sauce thickens, and the flavors intensify.
8. Now, let's bring in the marinara sauce and give it a good fold into the pan. Taste that goodness! If it's a tad too salty, don't worry. Just add ½ cup of water and taste again. If it needs a little more salt, sprinkle in ½ tsp and give it another taste.
9. Time to slice those sausages into ½ inch rounds and reunite them with the pan. Make sure they're well incorporated into the sauce, creating a symphony of flavors that will make your taste buds sing!
10. Lower the flame and let everything simmer on low until it's heated through. This is the moment when all the flavors meld together into pure bliss.

Get ready to savor the fusion of Italian and Puerto Rican goodness that awaits you. This dish is all about coming together, celebrating family traditions, and delighting in every flavorful bite. Gather your loved ones, serve it up with a side of warm smiles, and enjoy the taste adventure!

Serves: 8 (along with other sides)

YUCA CON MOJITO
"Cassava With Garlic Infused Oil"

Get ready to transport your taste buds to Puerto Rico with this delicious Yuca con Mojito recipe! I remember the days when I used to dine at "El Verde" in Rio Grande, savoring their mouthwatering Yuca with Mojito (infused garlic oil). The Yuca was soft, and the garlic oil was downright heavenly. After researching numerous recipes, I've landed on my favorite version of this Puerto Rican staple. You can find Yuca prepared like this all across the island, and let me tell you, it's beyond good!

Here's what you'll need:

Ingredients:
- 2.5 lbs. of Yuca*
- 1 tsp of salt for water

*Pro tip: Goya sells frozen Yuca, which works wonderfully for this recipe.

Let's dive into the magic of Yuca con Mojito:
1. Start by boiling water and adding 1 tsp of salt. Taste the water—it should have a nice salty kick. Add the Yuca to the boiling water, whether it's frozen or fresh. Let it cook until it becomes wonderfully soft and easily pricked with a fork. Oh, the anticipation!
2. Once the Yuca is cooked to perfection, remove the root from the middle of the Yuca pieces, if they have any. It looks like a white stick, so keep an eye out for it. Set the Yuca aside in a bowl and get ready for the star of the show—the Mojito Oil!
3. Grab your trusty pilon (mortar and pestle) and add 6 medium size garlic cloves and ¼ tsp of Adobo or salt. Mash them together, releasing those aromatic flavors. This is where the magic starts to happen.
4. In a cold frying pan, pour in 3 oz of olive oil and add the mashed garlic. We need to treat the garlic with love, so cook it over low heat, ensuring it doesn't burn. We want to extract all that wonderful garlicky essence.
5. Now, it's time to add one slice of Spanish onion, finely chopped, to the pan. Mix it in and keep the heat low. We're waiting for the onion to soften and release its sweet flavors, while being careful not to let the garlic burn. Slow and steady wins the race!
6. Take a moment to taste the oil and check its saltiness. Adjust as needed because we want that perfect balance of flavors. And voila! Your Mojito Oil is now ready to bring the Yuca to life!
7. Drizzle the tantalizing Mojito Oil all over your cooked Yuca, making sure every piece gets its fair share of flavor. The aroma will make your mouth water in anticipation.
8. For the finishing touch, sprinkle some fresh parsley over the Yuca. It adds a lovely pop of color and freshness, making your dish even more enticing.

Prepare to indulge in the exquisite flavors of Puerto Rico with every bite of this Yuca con Mojito. It's a dish that captures the essence of the island and leaves you craving more. So, gather your loved ones, dive into this culinary delight, and let the flavors transport you to the beautiful shores of Puerto Rico! ¡Buen provecho!

Serves: 5

STEAK SMOTHERED WITH ONIONS
Bistec Encebollado

Get ready for a culinary adventure as we dive into the world of Puerto Rican flavors! If you've read my first book, "Cooking and Telling Stories y El Pilon," you might remember the hilarious mishap that led this special Puerto Rican dish to end up in the garbage! But fear not, because I've perfected my own version of this mouthwatering staple that will leave you craving more.

Get your taste buds ready for this delicious Puerto Rican Cubed Steak with Vinegar Sauce. It's a dish where the vinegar takes the spotlight, so be prepared to taste often and ensure that the sauce has that savory vinegary flavor we all love. This recipe holds a special place in my heart, as it's a tribute to my mother's cooking that I adored.

Here's what you'll need for this flavor-packed adventure:

Ingredients:

For the Dry Rub (marinade the day before):
- 2 lbs. of Cubed Steak (approximately 5 pieces or 4 big pieces)
- ½ tsp of adobo (you might need to add more, but let's start with just ½ tsp)
- 1 tsp of garlic powder
- ½ tsp of oregano
- ½ tsp of smoked paprika
- ¼ tsp of onion powder
- 1 tbs of parsley
- 1 envelope of sazón
- 1 tsp of soy sauce (special ingredient)

In Pilon (mortar and pestle):
- Mash 3 garlic cloves
- ¼ tsp of adobo
- 3 tbs of oil
- 1 tbs of vinegar (make sure to taste first to achieve the perfect salt and vinegar balance)

Next Day Instructions:
1. Run the cubed steak under cold water until light blood is dripping from the steak. Properly dry the steak with paper towels, ensuring it's nice and dry.
2. Place the steaks in a large bowl for seasoning. Add the dry rub ingredients and the garlic sauce we prepared in the Pilon. Here's the key—taste the sauce! It should have a delightful vinegary tang without being overpowering. Adjust the seasoning as needed to suit your taste buds.
3. Slice the onion into rings (not too thin) and incorporate it well into the steak and marinade. Let those flavors mingle and dance together!
4. Seal your bowl and let the steaks marinate overnight in the refrigerator, allowing all the flavors to meld together beautifully. Trust me, patience will be rewarded!

Cooking the Steaks:
1. Heat a 12" frying pan over medium heat and add 2 tbs of olive oil. It's time to work some magic in the kitchen!
2. Add the marinated steaks to the pan one at a time, sizzling away with excitement. Pour in the remaining marinade, infusing the dish with even more flavor.
3. If additional liquid is required during cooking, start with ¼ cup of beef stock. This will help the steaks simmer gently under a very low flame for one hour. The liquid doesn't need to cover the steaks entirely but keep an eye on it to prevent evaporation. Keep some beef stock close by, just in case it's needed.
4. As the steaks simmer and soak up all the deliciousness, sprinkle some fresh cilantro leaves over them. This adds that quintessential Puerto Rican flavor and brings the dish to a whole new level of yum!
5. After one hour of simmering, give your sauce a taste test. Feel free to adjust the seasoning with a touch of adobo or oregano, adding that final burst of flavor to make it truly unforgettable.

Now that you've created this culinary masterpiece, it's time to serve it up! Pair your Puerto Rican Cubed Steak with Vinegar Sauce with fragrant white rice and beans, along with a refreshing salad and a slice of avocado. Get ready to savor the incredible flavors and embark on a culinary journey that celebrates the vibrant essence of Puerto Rico.

Buen provecho, and don't forget to share your delightful story of this dish with your loved ones at the dinner table!

Serves: 4

CHICKEN SCARPARIELLO A LA CLARI

Get ready for a culinary adventure that combines the best of both worlds! It all started when I wanted to cook chicken fricassee but realized I didn't have enough chicken pieces. But wait! An idea sparked in my mind as I glanced into my fridge and spotted a package of sweet Italian sausages. That's when the magic happened, I decided to infuse my sausage and peppers recipe with the flavors of chicken fricassee. Brace yourself for a taste sensation like no other!

Ingredients:

For the Chicken Fricassee:
- 4 chicken thighs (marinated overnight, see dry rub below)
- 1 package of sweet Italian sausages (about six links), sliced into rounds and set aside.
- ¼ cup of julienned red pepper
- ¼ cup of sliced julienned onion
- Garlic Sauce: two large cloves of garlic mashed in a pilon with 1/8 tsp of adobo, 4 tablespoons of olive oil, and 1 tablespoon of apple cider vinegar.
- 2 tablespoons of diced red pimientos (find in the Goya section)
- 1 tablespoon of oregano
- ¼ cup of merlot wine (because we're adding some special flair)
- 1 ½ cups of chicken stock
- ½ cup of chicken stock mixed with 2 tablespoons of flour
- ¼ cup of prepared tomato spaghetti sauce (any flavor works)
- Parmesan cheese (to sprinkle over the dish)

Dry Rub (marinade for chicken):
- In a small bowl, combine the following ingredients:
    - 1 envelope of sazón
    - 2 teaspoons of garlic powder
    - 1 teaspoon of oregano
    - ½ teaspoon of onion powder
    - ¼ teaspoon of smoked paprika
    - ¼ teaspoon of black pepper
    - 1 teaspoon of thyme
- Drizzle olive oil over the seasoned chicken, cover, and let it marinate overnight.

Instructions:
1. In a large frying pan, heat the garlic sauce over medium heat. Be careful not to burn the garlic—it should sizzle and release its aromatic fragrance.
2. Add the sliced Italian sausages and chicken pieces to the pan along with the oregano. Brown the meat on both sides, allowing the flavors to develop and create a delightful, caramelized crust.
3. Once the meat is nicely browned, it's time to add the red pepper, onion, and diced pimientos. Let them join the party, infusing the dish with their vibrant colors and flavors.

4. Pour in the merlot wine and give everything a good mix, ensuring that the ingredients are well-coated and mingling harmoniously.
5. Now, it's time to add the chicken stock and the chicken stock mixed with flour. This will create a luscious, savory sauce that will coat the meat and vegetables perfectly.
6. Stir in the ¼ cup of tomato sauce, adding a touch of richness and depth to the dish.
7. Cover the pan, reduce the heat to low (setting 3), and let it simmer for one hour. During this time, the flavors will meld together, creating a tantalizing aroma that will make your kitchen feel like a five-star restaurant.
8. Once the cooking is complete, serve this delightful creation over pasta or rice, allowing the flavors to mingle with the grains and create a symphony of taste. And don't forget the final touch—sprinkle some Parmesan cheese over the dish, adding a delightful burst of flavor and enhancing the overall experience.

Get ready to savor every bite of this unique fusion dish that combines the comforting flavors of chicken fricassee with the savory goodness of sausage and peppers. It's a culinary masterpiece that will transport your taste buds to new heights of deliciousness. Enjoy this incredible creation, with white rice, a slice of avocado, and don't forget to share the story of how it came to be with your family and friends as you gather around the table. Buon appetito!

Serves: 6

PORK COUNTRY RIBS COOKED IN AIR FRYER

Get ready to unleash the power of your air fryer with this unbelievably quick and delicious recipe for savory pork country ribs! It's 2023, and many households have embraced the wonders of air fryers. These ribs will taste like you spent hours roasting them in the oven, but the process is quick and easy. Get ready to savor every bite of these mouthwatering ribs!

Ingredients:
- 10 pieces of pork country ribs

Dry Rub:
- 1 tsp of adobo
- 2 tsp of garlic powder
- 1 tsp of oregano
- ½ tsp of smoked paprika
- ½ tsp of onion powder
- 1 envelope of sazón
- 2 tbsp of lite soy sauce (our special ingredient)

Makes 4 servings.

Let's get cooking!

1. Start by giving your ribs a refreshing rinse under cold water. Add a splash of vinegar to the water for an extra touch of cleanliness. Rinse the ribs once again under cold water and pat them dry thoroughly with paper towels.
2. Place the ribs in a large rectangle aluminum pan, ready for seasoning.
3. In a bowl, combine all the ingredients for the dry rub. Sprinkle the dry rub over the ribs and mix it thoroughly with your hands, ensuring each rib is generously coated. The aroma alone will make your taste buds dance!
4. Now, it's time to add a special twist. Grab a brush and spread the lite soy sauce over all the ribs, adding a delightful umami flavor to the mix.
5. Cover the aluminum pan tightly with aluminum foil, sealing in all the savory goodness. Place the pan in the refrigerator and let the ribs marinate overnight. Patience is key, but the wait will be worth it!

Cooking the Ribs in the Air Fryer:
1. Preheat your air fryer to 370 or 400 degrees Fahrenheit, depending on the intensity you desire.
2. Carefully arrange 4 ribs in the air fryer, ensuring they have enough space for optimal cooking. It's important not to overcrowd them.

3. Let the air fryer work its magic! Cook the ribs for 10 minutes, then flip them over and continue cooking for an additional 10 minutes. The sizzling sounds and tantalizing aromas will have your mouth watering in anticipation.
4. Once the cooking time is up, take out the perfectly air-fried ribs. They should be golden brown, juicy, and packed with flavor.

Serve and Enjoy:

Now that your savory pork country ribs are ready to be devoured, it's time to think about the perfect accompaniments. These delicious ribs pair well with a refreshing salad, zesty potato salad, or creamy mashed potatoes. Get creative with your sides and enjoy a complete and satisfying meal.

Get ready to dig in and enjoy the incredible taste and texture of these air-fried pork country ribs. They're the perfect way to savor a delightful meal without spending hours in the kitchen. Embrace the wonders of your air fryer and make each bite a burst of flavor and fun!

PASTELES UNTRADITIONAL PUERTO RICAN STYLE

During the challenging times of the pandemic, we were compelled to find innovative ways to celebrate the holidays while being unable to gather together. Here's a delightful approach to transforming the traditional process of making pasteles into a thrilling and solitary adventure! By making a few adjustments and adding a touch of lively Puerto Rican folk music to keep you inspired, you'll embark on a remarkable journey of preparing this cherished dish all on your own. And the best part? No more hassles with boiling, cutting strings, or risking burnt fingers. Get ready to groove to the beat and relish the experience with this fresh and exhilarating method of making pasteles.

So, put on your dancing shoes, gather your ingredients, and let the rhythm guide you through this festive pasteles-making experience. With each step, let the music and your love for cooking infuse the dish with an extra dose of excitement.

COOKED PASTELES

Ingredients:
- Pastele filling of your choice (traditional options include pork, chicken, or vegetable fillings), But for this recipe, pork was the selection.
- Aluminum foil
- 9 x 14 rectangular pan
- Larger Rectangular pan with water to hold the 9 x 14 pan comfortably. (a water-bath)
- 2 Yautias (taro root)
- 10 Green Bananas
- 1 Green Plantano (plantain)
- ½ Small Calabaza (pumpkin)
- 1 small piece of malanga (2-inch round) (optional)
- 1 Idaho Potato
- ½ cup of Achiote Seeds
- 1 cup of corn oil
- 2 tbs of adobo
- 2 cups of sauce from pork stew
- 2 large plantain leaves (optional), cleaned and prepared (softened over the stove, rinsed with running water, and pat dried

1. To infuse the oil with achiote flavor and give it a vibrant orange color, heat up the one cup of corn oil in a small saucepan. Add the ½ cup of achiote seeds and bring to a boil. Turn off the heat and set the pan aside to cool. Once cooled, strain the oil and set it aside.
2. Now it's time to get your hands dirty and have some fun! Take the yautias, green bananas, green plantain, calabaza, and malanga (if using) and finely grind them by hand until you form a dumpling-like mixture. As you mix, add 2 tbs of adobo, but do it gradually, tasting the dumpling along the way to ensure the perfect saltiness.
3. Slowly add the infused achiote oil until you have a beautiful orange color.
4. Add 2 cups of the flavorful sauce from the pork stew to the dumpling mixture and mix well. Let the aroma of the ingredients and the lively music inspire your movements.

This is how you prepare the pork Stew:
- Pork (Marinate overnight)
- 2 lbs. of pork chops (cut into cubes)
- 1 tsp sazón
- 2 tsp of garlic
- ½ tsp of oregano
- ½ tsp of onion powder
- ¼ tsp of cumin
- ¼ tsp of smoked paprika
- 1 tsp of soy sauce
- Drizzle of olive oil

Next day (Making Pork Stew). Let's spice up the process!
- 2 tbs of olive oil in a pot.
- ½ of medium yellow onion, diced

- 3 garlic cloves, mashed.
- ½ of red pepper, diced
- ¼ cup of chopped roasted red pepper (add after chicken stock is added)
- ¼ cup of fresh cilantro, chopped
- 1 tsp of Oregano leaves
- ½ cup of tomato sauce
- 2 packets of sazón
- 5 tbs of Sofrito (Goya makes this product)
- 2 to 3 cups of chicken stock
- 1 capful of apple cidar vinegar
- 8 oz of chickpeas (garbanzos) (without liquid) (add after chicken stock is added)

Now, let's prepare the pork stew.

1. In a pot, heat 2 tablespoons of olive oil. Sauté the diced yellow onion, mashed garlic cloves, diced red pepper, chopped roasted red pepper, and fresh cilantro. Add oregano leaves, tomato sauce, sazón, and the marinated pork. Cook until the pork is no longer pink.
2. Pour in 2 to 3 cups of chicken stock and add apple cider vinegar and drained chickpeas (garbanzos).
3. Ensure that the liquid level is about 1 inch above the meat. If needed, add an additional ½ cup of chicken stock. Bring the stew to a boil,
4. Then lower the heat and let it simmer for one hour. Keep an eye on the stew to prevent it from drying up.
5. Turn on the oven to 400 degrees.
6. Put on some lively SALSA music to set the mood and keep you entertained while you work. Let the vibrant beats and rhythmic melodies fuel your culinary creativity.
7. Instead of making individual pasteles, we're going to transform this dish into a delicious casserole-style creation. Prepare the pasteles filling of your choice, using traditional ingredients and spices that make this dish so special.
8. Lay down a layer of banana leaves in the bottom of your 9 x 14 rectangular pan. These leaves not only add flavor but also create an authentic touch to your dish.
9. Spoon a generous amount of the pastele dough filling onto the banana leaf layer, spreading it evenly to cover the entire surface of the pan.
10. Spoon a generous amount of pork stew on top of the pastele dough. Don't worry the stew won't sink!
11. Spoon another generous amount of the pastele dough onto top of the stew covering the entire stew.
12. Now take your ladle and add some of that wonderful stew liquid on top of the dough!
13. Add another layer of banana leaves on top of the filling, creating a lasagna-like effect.
14. This will help infuse the dish with the distinct aroma and flavors of the banana leaves.
15. Cover the pan tightly with aluminum foil, sealing in all the mouthwatering goodness. The foil will lock in the flavors and keep everything moist and tender.
16. Place water in a separate pan where you will place your aluminum foiled casserole pan.
17. Bake the pasteles in the oven at 400 degrees for two hours, allowing the flavors to meld together and the dough to cook through.

18. While the pasteles casserole bakes, feel free to dance and sing along to the lively Puerto Rican music. Let the rhythm inspire your inner chef and make the cooking process an enjoyable experience.
19. Once the pasteles casserole is cooked to perfection, remove it from the oven and let it cool for a few minutes. The anticipation builds as the delightful aromas waft through the air.
20. With a smile on your face and a bounce in your step, cut the pasteles casserole into neat squares, ready to be plated and served. Each square holds a piece of Puerto Rican culinary heritage and your personal touch.
21. As you savor the delicious flavors of your pasteles creation, let the joy of your solo culinary adventure fill your heart. You've transformed a labor-intensive dish into a fun and enjoyable experience, all while preserving the essence of Puerto Rican cuisine.

¡Buen provecho y a bailar!

Serves: 8

Meatballs with Pasta

Let's turn this recipe into a fun and memorable cooking experience! Get ready to bring out your inner chef and add a touch of excitement to the process. Here we go:

Ingredients:
- 1 Box of Penne Pasta
- 2 24 oz bottles of Bertolli Vineyard Marinara Tomato Sauce
- ¼ cup of Merlot Wine
- 2.25 lbs. Ground beef
- 1 tbs of Olive Oil

Now, let's make this cooking adventure more enjoyable!
1. Put on your favorite upbeat playlist or turn up the volume on your favorite cooking show. Let the lively tunes or the enthusiastic hosts inspire and energize you throughout the cooking process.
2. Gather all your ingredients and create a cooking station that reflects your creativity. Arrange the ingredients in colorful bowls and have them ready to use.
3. Instead of just sprinkling the seasoning on the ground beef, let's add a twist. Imagine you're a professional chef on a cooking show, and it's time for the dramatic "seasoning reveal." Sprinkle the oregano, garlic powder, Sazón Goya, Goya Chicken Bouillon, and onion powder onto the ground beef with a flourish. Enjoy the anticipation of the flavors blending.
4. Carefully turn the ground beef over and repeat the seasoning process on the other side. Take a moment to appreciate the beautiful colors and aromas coming together.
5. Now, it's time to elevate the mixing process. Put on a fun apron, roll up your sleeves, and mix the ground beef and the remaining ingredients with your hands. Embrace the tactile experience and enjoy the feeling of the ingredients coming together.
6. As you shape the mixture into round meatballs, envision yourself competing in a cooking challenge. Try to make them as uniform and visually appealing as possible. Let your creativity shine!
7. Heat up a large pot and add a touch of olive oil. Get ready to put your browning skills to the test. Place the meatballs in the pot and let them sizzle. Imagine you're showcasing your browning technique on a cooking show, impressing the judges with your culinary skills.
8. Once the meatballs are nicely browned, carefully remove them from the pot. Feel a sense of accomplishment as you admire your perfectly browned meatballs.
9. Drain most of the oil from the pot but leave a little for added flavor. It's time to add the star of the show: the tomato sauce. Open the bottles of Bertolli Vineyard Marinara Tomato Sauce with a flourish, pouring them into the pot over low heat. Take a moment to enjoy the rich aroma of the simmering sauce.
10. Gently place the meatballs back into the pot, ensuring they are submerged in the delicious sauce. Sprinkle a pinch of oregano on top for that extra touch of flavor. Remember, presentation matters even in your own kitchen!

11. Pour in the merlot wine, imagining that you're a sommelier pairing the perfect wine with your culinary creation. Let the flavors mingle and simmer together for 30 minutes over low heat. Take this time to dance around the kitchen or share funny anecdotes with your loved ones.
12. Cook your favorite pasta according to the package instructions. As the pasta cooks, let the mouthwatering aroma of the sauce and meatballs fill your kitchen, building anticipation for the final dish.
13. Once the pasta is al dente, drain it and serve it on a colorful platter. Now, it's time to bring the dish together! Picture yourself as a food stylist, artfully arranging the meatballs and sauce on top of the pasta, creating a visually stunning presentation.
14. Take a moment to admire your culinary masterpiece. Capture a picture or invite your family and friends to gather around the table. Share stories, laughter, and enjoy the company of loved ones as you savor the flavors of your homemade creation.
15. Don't forget to clean up while keeping the joyful spirit alive. Sing along to your favorite cleaning-themed song or dance with the broom as you tidy up the kitchen. Celebrate the fun you had during this cooking adventure!

Remember, cooking is not only about the delicious food but also about the joy, creativity, and connection it brings. Embrace the fun in the kitchen and let your culinary adventures be filled with laughter and memorable moments. Enjoy every bite and savor the satisfaction of creating something special!

Serves: 6

SWEET POTATO CASSEROLE

Get ready to enjoy this delightful dish and create unforgettable memories. Here's how to make it more fun:

Ingredients:
- 3.5 lbs. Orange Sweet Potatoes
- 2 eggs – room temperature
- ¾ cup of packed brown sugar
- ½ tsp of cinnamon
- 1 tsp of vanilla extract
- 1 tsp of salt
- ¼ cup of melted unsalted butter (1 stick)
- 2 tbs dark rum (optional)

For the Crumble:
- 1 cup of brown sugar
- 2/3 cup of flour
- 6 tbs of cold butter

Now, let's add some fun to the process:
1. Turn on your favorite upbeat music or create a Thanksgiving cooking playlist. Dance and sing along as you gather the ingredients and prepare for your sweet potato casserole adventure.
2. As the sweet potatoes bake, engage in some friendly competition. Challenge your loved ones to a sweet potato peeling race. Set up separate stations with pre-baked sweet potatoes, peelers, and bowls. See who can peel their sweet potatoes the fastest and with the least amount of skin left behind. The winner gets a small prize or bragging rights for the day.
3. Once the sweet potatoes are cooled and mashed, encourage everyone to gather around and take turns adding the remaining ingredients. Make it a team effort and pass the mixing bowl around, allowing each person to contribute to the creamy and flavorful mixture. Take silly photos or videos during the process to capture the fun-filled moments.
4. Now it's time for the crumble topping. Instead of simply mixing the ingredients, challenge your loved ones to a crumble design contest. Provide various small bowls and let everyone create their unique crumble designs using the brown sugar, flour, and cold butter. The most creative and visually appealing design wins the title of "Master Crumble Artist."
5. Before placing the casserole in the oven, invite your family or friends to write down one thing they're grateful for on small slips of paper. Collect the gratitude notes and place them in a jar. As the casserole bakes, take turns reading and sharing the messages of gratitude, fostering a sense of warmth and appreciation.
6. Once the casserole is beautifully baked and golden, gather around the table and appreciate the masterpiece you've created together. Take turns serving the casserole to each person, adding an extra dollop of whipped cream or a sprinkle of cinnamon on top. Share stories, laughter, and gratitude as you savor each bite of the delectable sweet potato casserole.

7. Don't forget to capture the final presentation of the casserole. Take photos or create a short cooking show-style video, complete with taste tests and reviews from your family and friends. Share your creations on social media or keep them as cherished memories.
8. Lastly, as you enjoy the sweet potato casserole, take a moment to express appreciation for the newfound popularity.

Bake Casserole 40 to 45 minutes @ 400 degrees.

Serves: 10

MARISA'S TOMATO SOUP

Get ready to embark on a fun cooking adventure with Marisa's delicious soup recipe! Let's turn up the excitement and make it a joyful experience:

I am bursting with pride because I taught Marisa how to cook, and now we're like culinary partners in crime! She recently shared an amazing soup recipe with me, and I was skeptical at first, but oh boy, was I in for a treat! This soup is a flavor explosion, with hints of smokiness, buttery goodness, and garlic stealing the show. It's a bit involved, but trust me, the outcome is worth it. Let's dive in!

Ingredients:
- 2.5 lbs. of tomatoes
- 1 yellow pepper
- 2 large onions
- A handful of fresh basil leaves
- 4 bulbs of garlic*
- 1 tsp of sugar
- Salt, Italian seasoning, and pepper to taste
- Olive oil to taste
- Balsamic vinegar to taste
- 1 envelope of sazón (our secret ingredient)
- 1 envelope of chicken bouillon (Goya)
- 1 cup of parmesan cheese
- ¼ cup of whipping cream
- A strainer
- An electric mixer (or food processor)

First things first, let's preheat the oven to 400°F. And while it's heating up, we'll work our magic with the garlic bulbs. Slice the tops off each garlic bulb and drizzle them generously with olive oil. Sprinkle some salt, pepper, and Italian seasoning on each bulb, then wrap them individually in aluminum foil, sealing them tight. Pop them in a small oven-safe tray and place them in the top part of the oven. Let the garlic bulbs roast for 45 minutes, and once done, let them cool completely before handling. Trust me, they'll be worth the wait!

Now, let's move on to the veggies. Chop up the tomatoes, onions, and yellow pepper, and spread them out on a flat baking sheet. Drizzle olive oil generously over the veggies and sprinkle them with salt, black pepper, Italian seasoning, and a dash of balsamic vinegar. We're going to give these a blast of heat, so place them in the 400°F oven for about 15 to 30 minutes, or until they're nicely roasted.

Once the veggies are done, remove them from the oven and turn off the heat. It's time to bring in the roasted garlic! Squeeze each bulb, and let that delicious garlicky goodness mingle with the roasted veggies. Give it a good mix with a spoon. Now, in batches, transfer the veggies to an electric mixer or food processor. Blend them until smooth and creamy. For an extra touch of perfection, strain the soup through a sieve, using a potato masher to squeeze out all that delicious juice/soup. Transfer the strained soup to a pot and place it on the stove over low heat.

Here comes the fun part! Add a teaspoon of sugar, a cup of parmesan cheese, and a quarter cup of whipping cream to the pot. Give it a good stir and get ready to taste the magic. If it needs a little extra kick, sprinkle in some sazón from the secret envelope. Taste again and adjust the saltiness if needed. If it's still calling for a little something-something, add half a packet of chicken bouillon. Taste one last time, and voila!

Remember, we don't want this soup to boil, so keep the heat low and steady. Now, grab some grill cheese or garlic bread, and get ready to indulge in this sensational soup creation. It's time to satisfy those taste buds and experience the joy of homemade deliciousness!

So put on your apron, grab your favorite cooking tunes, and let the kitchen adventure begin. Enjoy every spoonful and savor the joy of cooking and sharing a meal made with love. Bon appétit!

Serves: 4

PUERTO RICAN SHRIMP STEW

Let's make this Puerto Rican shrimp stew even more fun and enjoyable! Get ready to have a blast cooking and savoring this savory dish. Here's how to add some excitement to your table surrounded by your friends:

Ingredients
- 1 lb. of shrimp, cleaned and deveined (save shrimp casings for broth)
- 1 cup of diced onion
- Half of a green pepper, diced.
- Half of a red pepper, diced.
- 2 tablespoons of sofrito
- 2 packets of Sazón seasoning
- 2 packets of chicken bouillon (for fish broth)
- 1/4 cup of tomato sauce
- 4 garlic cloves, mashed.
- 1/2 cup of chopped cooking ham
- 1/2 cup of uncooked rice (soak in water for 4 hours)
- 8 cups of water
- Fresh cilantro for garnish
- Oil for frying
- Plantains for frying (to serve as a side dish)

For the Fish Broth:
1. In a pot, combine the shrimp casings, a bunch of fresh cilantro, 1 packet of Sazón seasoning, and 2 envelopes of chicken bouillon.
2. Add water (approximately 4 cups) to the pot and bring it to a boil.
3. Simmer for about 15-20 minutes to infuse the flavors into the broth.
4. Strain the broth and set it aside for later use.

For the Shrimp and Rice Dish:
1. In another pot, heat 2 tablespoons of oil.
2. Add the cooking ham and sauté it for a few minutes.
3. Add the diced onions, mashed garlic cloves, sofrito, and diced peppers to the pot. Cook until the vegetables become translucent.
4. Stir in 1 packet of Sazón seasoning and the tomato sauce. Continue to sauté for a few more minutes.
5. Add the shrimp to the pot and cook until they turn pink. Remove about 3/4 of the cooked shrimp and set them aside.

6. Pour in the fish broth and add an additional 4 cups of water. Taste the broth and adjust the salt if necessary. You can add more chicken bouillon or salt, as desired.
7. Drain the soaked rice and add it to the pot. Cook for approximately 25 minutes or until the rice is tender.
8. Once the rice is cooked, add the reserved cooked shrimp back into the pot and simmer for an additional 5 minutes to allow the flavors to meld together. So Savory!

For the Fried Plantains:
1. Peel and slice the plantains into thin pieces.
2. Heat oil in a separate pan for frying.
3. Fry the plantain slices until golden brown.
4. Press each plantain until flat, refry until crispy.
5. Remove the fried plantains from the oil and drain them on a paper towel.

To serve: Plate the shrimp and rice dish, garnish with fresh cilantro, and serve with the fried plantains on the side.

Remember to taste the dish as you add ingredients and adjust the seasoning according to your preference. Enjoy your Puerto Rican-style shrimp and rice with a side of crispy fried plantains and a huge slice of avocado! Simply mouth-watering!

Serves: 4 (Large Soup Bowls or 8 Small Soup Bowls)

BREADED BREAST OF CHICKEN

Get ready to take your chicken game to the next level with this savory breaded chicken breast recipe! Let's infuse it with greatness and make the cooking process a fun and delicious experience:

Ingredients:
- 1 boneless chicken breast
- 1 paring knife
- ½ tsp of adobo seasoning
- 1 tsp of garlic powder
- ½ tsp of oregano leaves
- ½ tsp of onion powder
- ½ tsp of smoked paprika
- 1 cup of Italian breadcrumbs
- 4 tbs of olive oil
- 1 tbs of butter

Now, let's dive into the flavorful journey of creating succulent chicken perfection:
1. Begin by rinsing the chicken breast under cold water. To add a special touch, sprinkle a bit of apple cider vinegar all over the chicken, then rinse it again under cold water. Dry the chicken thoroughly with a paper towel.
2. Grab your trusty paring knife and carefully slice the chicken breast into approximately 4 pieces. Take your time and handle the knife with precision.
3. It's time to season the chicken and make it truly extraordinary. In a gallon-size storage bag, combine the adobo seasoning, garlic powder, oregano leaves, onion powder, and smoked paprika. Give the bag a gentle shake to mix the seasonings. Place the sliced chicken breast pieces into the bag and coat them thoroughly with the flavorful seasoning. Let the chicken marinate and soak up all the goodness.
4. Get ready to coat the chicken with the crispy breadcrumbs. In a separate dish, spread out the Italian breadcrumbs. Take each seasoned chicken slice from the bag and carefully coat it with the breadcrumbs, making sure to cover all sides. Place the breaded chicken slices on a clean plate, ready to be cooked to perfection.
5. It's time to fire up the stove and bring out the sizzle! In a pan, add the olive oil and butter, then heat it up over medium heat. Wait until the oil and butter mixture is hot and ready to work its magic.
6. Carefully add each breaded chicken breast slice to the pan, savoring the delightful sizzling sound. Fry the chicken for about 4 minutes on each side, or until the edges turn a beautiful golden brown. Flip them over with confidence and let the other side cook to perfection.
7. Once the chicken breasts are cooked to succulent and savory perfection, remove them from the pan and place them on a clean plate. Get creative with your plating and pair them with a fresh salad or some comforting rice and beans. Let your culinary imagination run wild!

Now, it's time to enjoy the fruits of your labor. Bite into that crispy, flavorful crust and savor the tender juiciness of the chicken. Don't forget to share this delightful dish with your loved ones and bask in the joy of creating a signature masterpiece. Happy cooking and buen provecho!

Serves: 5

COOKING WHITE RICE

Get ready to conquer the world of cooking perfect white rice with the guidance of your sweet grandma! Let's turn this rice-cooking adventure into a fun and foolproof experience:

First, let's gather our ingredients and prepare to unlock the secrets of consistent white rice perfection:

Medium Grain Rice:
- 1 cup of uncooked rice
- 1 ½ cups of water
- 1 tablespoon of olive oil

Long Grain Rice or Jasmine Rice:
- 1 cup of uncooked rice
- 2 cups of water
- 2 tablespoons of olive oil

Now, let the rice-cooking fun begin:
1. Choose your rice adventure! Depending on whether you're cooking medium grain rice or long grain/Jasmine rice, the water-to-rice ratio will differ. Grandma's tip is to always use the same cup to measure both the rice and the water, ensuring consistency and perfect results.
2. If you're using a traditional stovetop method, grab a saucepan or pot and let's get cooking. Add the measured rice to the pot and rinse it under cold water to remove any excess starch.
3. Drain the rice thoroughly and place it back into the pot. Now, it's time to add the liquid love that will transform the rice into a fluffy masterpiece. For medium grain rice, add 1 ½ cups of water. For long grain or Jasmine rice, use 2 cups of water. Drizzle in the olive oil, which adds a touch of richness and flavor to the rice.
4. It's time to bring the pot to life! Place it on the stovetop over medium heat and let it come to a gentle boil. Once it reaches a boil, reduce the heat to low and cover the pot with a well-fitted lid.
5. Let the rice work its magic and cook undisturbed for the designated time. For medium grain rice, let it simmer for approximately 15-20 minutes. For long grain or Jasmine rice, allow it to cook for around 20-25 minutes. Remember, no peeking allowed during this process!
6. As the aroma of perfectly cooked rice fills the air, resist the temptation to uncover the pot. Instead, turn off the heat and let the rice rest for about 5 minutes. This step allows the steam to redistribute and helps create that ideal fluffiness we all desire.
7. Finally, it's time to uncover the pot and reveal your culinary masterpiece. Take a fork or rice paddle and gently fluff the rice, separating the grains and releasing the built-up steam. Marvel at the perfectly cooked rice that awaits you.

Now, whether you're enjoying a traditional stovetop preparation or using a trusty rice cooker, remember to follow the same measurements and ratio for rice and water. Embrace the adventure of creating consistently delicious white rice, just as your grandma taught you. You can add salt to your rice but since it will certainly be paired with a protein the protein adds the salt.

Serves: 2

TASTY MINI CHEESECAKES
The perfect bite when craving something sweet and delicious!

Get ready for a delightful treat that will satisfy your sweet tooth without the guilt! These mini cheesecakes are not only incredibly tasty but also easy to make. Indulge in the creamy goodness and take your sweet tooth to new levels of satisfaction. Let's get started and have some fun!

Ingredients:

Crust:
- ¾ cup of Graham Crackers Crumbs (about 6 whole crackers)
- 1 ½ tablespoons of Sugar
- 3 tablespoons of unsalted butter (melted)
- Pinch of Salt

Filling:
- 2 packages (8 oz each) of cream cheese (softened)
- ½ cup of sugar
- 1 teaspoon of vanilla extract
- 2 eggs (medium) at room temperature
- ¼ cup of sour cream
- ½ teaspoon of Liquor 43 or Bacardi Coconut Rum (our special ingredient)
- 2 teaspoons of lemon zest
- Pinch of Salt

Topping*:
- 8 strawberries, sliced.
- Juice of half an orange (another special ingredient)
- 1 teaspoon of sugar
- Whipped Cream (add when serving) *Prepare the strawberries ahead of time and place them in the refrigerator to chill properly. DO NOT ADD WHIPPED CREAM YET.

Serves 12 mini cheesecakes.

Instructions:
1. Preheat the oven to 325°F.
2. Use a 12-count muffin pan and line each muffin tin with cupcake paper liners.
3. Let's prepare the crust. Break the graham crackers into a one-gallon plastic zip-lock bag until you achieve a crumb consistency. Add sugar and salt. Pour in the melted butter and mix well until the crumbs are well blended.

4. Evenly distribute the cracker crumbs into each liner and press them down using a ¼ cup measuring cup to create a crust. Set aside.
5. Now, let's prepare the filling. Place the softened cream cheese in a mixing bowl and mix it by hand or with an electric mixer on low speed.
6. In a separate bowl, add 2 teaspoons of lemon zest to the sugar and mix them together using a fork until well blended.
7. Gradually add the lemon zest sugar mixture to the cream cheese, blending it well.
8. Add the vanilla extract and the special ingredient, Liquor 43 or Bacardi Coconut Rum, for an extra kick of flavor.
9. Crack each egg into a separate bowl and mix with a fork before adding it to the cream cheese mixture. Mix each egg in separately and only until it is incorporated into the cream cheese. Avoid overmixing.
10. Fold in the sour cream gently.
11. Transfer the filling into a one-gallon zip-lock bag, then cut a very small hole in one corner. Pour the filling evenly into each muffin tin, filling them halfway. Take your time and enjoy the process.
12. Place the muffin pan on the middle rack of the oven and bake for 18 to 20 minutes. The cheesecakes will puff up and then settle down as they bake. They are done when the centers are almost set.
13. Turn off the oven, open the door, and let the cheesecakes cool for 30 minutes inside the oven.
14. Remove the muffin pan from the oven and let the cheesecakes cool completely.
15. Refrigerate the mini cheesecakes until they are completely chilled.
16. When you are ready to serve, prepare the topping. In a bowl, combine the sliced strawberries, orange juice, and sugar to create a luscious fruity topping.
17. Add a spoonful of the strawberry mixture (or just whipped cream) to each mini cheesecake when serving. This will give your mini cheesecakes an elegant and delicious touch!

Now it's time to enjoy these delightful mini cheesecakes with their irresistible crust, creamy filling, and tantalizing topping. Share them with your loved ones and savor every bite of this guilt-free indulgence!

Arroz con Dulce
(Rice Pudding)

Get ready to embark on a rice pudding adventure filled with culture and family traditions! Rice pudding, believed to have originated in China or India, holds a special place in many households, including mine. My mother's warm and gooey rice pudding during the holidays was a treat I always looked forward to. And let me tell you about the legendary rice pudding recipe I received from Margie Hernandez, Dickie's late sister. It has become a family favorite, and I can't wait to share it with you. Get ready to create this very special dessert!

Ingredients:

Ingredients for the Tea:
- 32 oz of water
- 6 sticks of cinnamon
- 12 cloves
- 4 slices of fresh ginger
- 1 tsp of anise seeds

Ingredients:
- Tea (prepared using the above ingredients)
- 2 cans of evaporated milk
- 2 cans of coconut milk
- 2 cans of cream of coconut
- 1 cup of milk
- 1 tsp of vanilla extract
- 4 tbsp of butter
- 1 cup of golden raisins
- 1/3 cup of Liquor 43 (our special ingredient)
- 1 cup of brown sugar (taste first before adding)
- 2 cups of medium-grain rice (soaked overnight in water)

Step One:
1. Let's start by making the tea. In a pot, combine the water, cinnamon sticks, cloves, fresh ginger slices, and anise seeds. Bring the mixture to a boil and let it simmer for 30 minutes. The tea should have a nice golden/brown color.

2. Strain the tea to remove the spices and ginger. Set aside the tea in a very large pot and return one cinnamon stick to the tea.

Step Two:
1. Place the pot with the tea over medium heat. Begin adding the evaporated milk, coconut milk, cream of coconut, and regular milk to the pot. Try to prevent the mixture from boiling; if it does, reduce the heat slightly.
2. Add the vanilla extract and butter to the pot.
3. Drain the water from the soaked rice and rinse the rice under cold water. Add the rice to the pot and stir continuously to prevent sticking and clumping.
4. Now it's time to add some extra flavor! Pour in 1/3 cup of Liquor 43 (or substitute with coconut rum) and the golden raisins. Stir the mixture for 5 minutes before adding the brown sugar. Remember to taste the mixture before adding the brown sugar to adjust the sweetness according to your preference.
5. At this stage, it may seem like there's a lot of liquid for just two cups of rice, but don't worry—the rice will absorb the liquid as it cooks. Be prepared for the mixture to boil rapidly and lower the heat if needed. It's best to cook the rice pudding at a very low temperature, like setting it to 3 on your stove. You want to avoid a rapid boil, so maintain a gentle simmer.
6. Keep stirring the mixture until it reaches the consistency of oatmeal. Once it reaches that point, turn off the heat and carefully drain the mixture into your desired pans. Remember to have your trays ready before you start cooking the rice pudding.

Note: You can use one large pan or several smaller pans, depending on your preference.

Congratulations! You've created a batch of delicious rice pudding filled with love and flavor. Now, all that's left to do is let it cool down. Once chilled, get ready to serve and share this delightful dessert with your loved ones. Enjoy the warm memories and the rich cultural heritage that comes with each spoonful of this special treat!

Serves: 15

COQUITO
(Puertorican Eggnog)

Last but not least, let's top off my culinary journey in Puerto Rico with the pièce de résistance— the process of making Coquito. Ah, Coquito, the quintessential holiday delight that brings joy to every gathering on this enchanting island. No Puerto Rican celebration is complete without the hostess raising a glass of freshly made Coquito for a toast. So, my friend, let's turn this Coquito making experience into an unforgettable, festive, and downright fun adventure! Get ready to immerse yourself in the holiday spirit and infuse your Coquito-making with a touch of excitement. Here's the recipe for a sensational Coquito experience:

Ingredients:
- 1 Electric Mixer
- Several clean empty bottles for Coquito
- 1 funnel
- 1 huge bowl
- 4 cans of evaporated milk
- 1 can of cream of coconut
- 1 can of condensed milk (7 oz)
- 6 egg yolks, medium size if possible
- ¼ teaspoon cinnamon powder
- ½ tsp of vanilla extract
- 1 cup of Liquor 43* (special ingredient). IF NOT AVAILABLE, USE 1 CUP OF COCONUT RUM
- ½ cup of black rum (Has to be Bacardi)
- ½ cup of coconut rum (Don Q, Bacardi, or Malibu)
- Cinnamon sticks to place in Coquito Bottles

Now, let's add some holiday cheer to the Coquito-making process:
1. Set the mood by playing your favorite holiday tunes or creating a Coquito-making playlist. Sing along and dance to the festive beats as you prepare the ingredients.
2. Gather your family or friends and turn the Coquito-making into a group activity. Assign fun roles like the Coquito mixer, the bottle filler, and the cinnamon stick decorator. Share laughs and create memories together.
3. As you add the ingredients to the electric mixer, encourage everyone to take turns mixing and blending the flavors. Make it a friendly competition to see who can create the smoothest and frothiest mixture.

4. When it's time to add the liquors, imagine you're a master mixologist crafting a signature holiday cocktail. Measure and pour the Liquor 43 or coconut rum with flair and confidence, celebrating the special touch they bring to the Coquito.
5. Before transferring the Coquito to the empty bottles, let everyone decorate their own bottle with festive ribbons, personalized labels, or colorful stickers. Encourage creativity and see who can come up with the most eye-catching design.
6. Once the bottles are ready, use the funnel to pour the Coquito into each bottle. Take turns and challenge each other to pour with precision and without spilling a drop. Make it a game and see who has the steadiest hand.
7. After the Coquito is safely stored in the bottles, take a moment to toast to the holiday season. Raise your beautifully decorated wine glasses filled with ice and a splash of Coquito. Make a joyful toast to good times, great company, and the delicious Coquito you've created together.
8. As you wait for the Coquito to mature in the fridge, plan a special Coquito tasting event. Invite friends or family over to sample the Coquito and share their thoughts. Create a cozy ambiance with twinkling lights, holiday decorations, and soft music in the background.
9. When it's time to taste the Coquito, serve it in elegant wine glasses and garnish each glass with a sprinkle of cinnamon. Encourage everyone to take small sips, savoring the flavors, and sharing their reactions. Compare notes and celebrate the success of your homemade Coquito.
10. Throughout the holiday season, whenever you enjoy a glass of Coquito, let it be a reminder of the joyful moments shared while making it. Raise your glass in celebration, toast to cherished memories, and let the delicious taste of Coquito transport you to the warmth and happiness of the holiday season.

Remember to drink responsibly and enjoy the Coquito in moderation. May your Coquito making adventure be filled with laughter, love, and the festive spirit! Cheers to a wonderful holiday season! Live Long and Prosper!

Serves: 6/Bottle

In conclusion, this Puerto Rican Cooking Book has been a labor of love, preserving the rich culinary heritage and vibrant flavors of Puerto Rico. Through its pages, we have embarked on a culinary journey, exploring traditional recipes passed down through generations, as well as innovative twists that reflect the evolving nature of Puerto Rican cuisine.

From the moment we embarked on this culinary adventure, we were transported to the bustling streets of Old San Juan, the vibrant markets brimming with fresh ingredients, and the warm kitchens filled with the aromas of sofrito, adobo, and sazón. We have delved into the diverse range of Puerto Rican dishes, from hearty stews like asopao and fricassees to the mouthwatering delights of desserts.

Throughout this book, we have celebrated the importance of food as a centerpiece of Puerto Rican culture, bringing families and communities together to share in the joy of a well-prepared meal. We have learned the art of the delicate balance of flavors in our beloved arroz con gandules.

But beyond the recipes themselves, this book has also shared the stories and memories that make Puerto Rican cuisine truly special. From the cherished family gatherings where grandmothers passed down their culinary wisdom, to the festive celebrations where the rhythmic beats of salsa and reggaeton were accompanied by plates piled high with delectable dishes.

It is my hope that this Puerto Rican Cooking Book has not only provided you with a collection of recipes but has also ignited your passion for the vibrant flavors and cultural heritage of Puerto Rico. May you be inspired to gather loved ones around the kitchen table, to create memories as you explore the diverse array of dishes within these pages.

Remember, cooking is an art, and each dish is an expression of love, creativity, and the spirit of Puerto Rico. So, grab your apron, gather your ingredients, and let the aromas and flavors transport you to the enchanting island that holds a special place in our hearts.

Enjoy your culinary journey through the flavors of Puerto Rico.

www.ingramcontent.com/pod-product-compliance
Lightning Source LLC
LaVergne TN
LVHW072129060526
838201LV00071B/5000